Fluffy the Apartment Cat

Fluffy the Apartment Cat

Anita Sutherland Millmann

VANTAGEPress
New York

Vantage Press and the Vantage Press colophon
are registered trademarks of Vantage Press, Inc.

FIRST EDITION

Copyright © 2009 by Anita Sutherland Millmann

Published by Vantage Press, Inc.
419 Park Ave. South, New York, NY 10016

Manufactured in the United States of America
ISBN: 978-0-533-16057-0

Library of Congress Catalog Card No: 2008904192

Printed in November 2010 in the United States of America by
The Covington Group in Kansas City, MO.

0 9 8 7 6 5 4 3 2 1

For Zita, who taught me trust and love.

Fluffy the Apartment Cat

Fluffy outside with his raccoon friends.

Many times I looked across the Puget Sound waters and dreamed about living on the other side of the huge bridge called The Narrows. Finally my dream came true and I moved across the bridge to a quaint, animal-friendly apartment community.

The small coastal town is just the right place for retirement and leisure living. Several marinas, lush green parks and small boutiques make it a great place for long walks.

I was enchanted with the animal-loving easygoing lifestyle in my new apartment community.

As I drove up to unload my belongings I noticed a red and white furry cat laying comfortably in the middle of the road. Later I saw the cat going to my next door neighbor's balcony to get some food. On a rainy day I saw the cat drink water from a gully. To my surprise I watched the cat sleep unafraid with raccoons at night. The raccoons seemed to accept the cat as it snuggled up.

My neighbor said the cat had been left behind by his owner when they moved out a year ago.

The cat has been fending for itself ever since. The neighbor said they felt sorry for the cat and began feeding it.

I said, "I would like to adopt the cat." The neighbor said she was happy about that because her family was moving back to Texas real soon.

The neighbor handed me cat food and some bowls. I started to feed the cat on my balcony but soon the cat came inside to eat. The cat sniffed around every room then laid down on a soft chair and fell asleep. The neighbor said it may be easy for the cat to come in since the former owner lived in my apartment before they moved.

Fluffy outside on the porch.

Fluffy in a makeshift outside bed.

Fluffy in bed inside.

I named the cat "Fluffy."

The veterinarian told me Fluffy is a boy cat and at least two years old. Fluffy made himself at home and pretty soon he slept in a bed, my bed to be exact. I gladly moved over for him.

On a cold windy fall day, twenty-four-year-old "Orange," Fluffy's older cat sister, ran out the door and into deep brush in thick woods near the apartment.

Nightfall came and I heard little crying sounds. Orange could not find her way out of the wilderness. I walked around the edge of the woods calling her name until midnight. One of the neighbors yelled out of his window, "Be quiet!"

Orange lost in the woods.

I forgot how late it had become and my neighbor had to sleep. I gave up calling her and went indoors. I looked at Fluffy and tearfully told him the problem with Orange. Fluffy looked at me with an intense facial expression as I spoke.

Fluffy then walked to the front door and scratched to go out. At first I did not want to open the door but Fluffy was very persistent, scratching again and again.

Finally I opened the door and as Fluffy walked out he stopped and looked at me.

It seemed he wanted me to follow him, so I did.

Fluffy walked to the wooded area and as we got close we could hear Orange cry. Fluffy disappeared into the brush. Minutes later Fluffy reappeared with Orange by his side. Orange was dirty and wet and shivering from the cold night air.

I picked Orange up and happily held her in my arms. Fluffy stood beside me. He looked proud and for a moment I thought he was smiling. I said, "Thank you, Fluffy, you are a hero."

From that day on I called Fluffy my search and rescue cat.

Fluffy has a baby cat brother named Harley. Harley loved sitting in a chair on the porch. One day Harley disappeared. On the evening of the fifth day I heard a faint "meow" in the night air. Fluffy sat next to me and perked up his ears. He heard the "meow" too. I looked at Fluffy and said "show me where Harley is."

Fluffy led me to a small slippery path in the woods. Fluffy jumped on a large fallen tree stump and stopped.

I said, "I can hear Harley cry but I cannot see him."

Fluffy raised his eyes and looked in a direction. I followed his gaze with my eyes and lo and behold there was Harley. He was high up in a tall tree, crying his eyes out.

I yelled "Harley!" Harley looked at me with panic in his eyes. I yelled "Hold on, I will help you!"

I noticed there were no branches on the lower part of the tree. The ground was slippery, getting close was very hard and my feet kept slipping out from under me. Fluffy stood there right by my side, looking up at Harley.

Harley and the big tree.

I thought about how to get him down from the tree. I said to Harley, "Turn around and lower yourself by clawing into the tree and I will catch you when you get low enough."

I could not believe my eyes. Harley turned around and started a slow backward descent by clawing into the tree.

When Harley had climbed down within two feet of my outstretched arms he suddenly let go of the tree and I caught him in midair as he dropped down. What a miracle!

Harley cuddled my neck as I took him home with Fluffy in tow. Harley was hungry and thirsty after so many days in the tree.

He recovered by eating big gulps of cat food and water. Afterward he laid down next to Fluffy and slept for a long time.

A couple of weeks later Fluffy desperately scratched on the balcony door and wanted to go outside. I was familiar now with his urgency. I opened the sliding door and Fluffy quickly ran down a small embankment and across the road. I watched him as he stopped in front of a gully opening. He began to circle the gully. What was he doing? I fearfully called out to him, "Fluffy, come back, do not go in there!"

The gully.

Kitty safely back home.

He entered the gully through its metal bars. Calling his name in worry, I ran to the gully in sheer panic. Suddenly Fluffy reappeared from in between the bars with a grey kitten in tow.

Once again Fluffy was on a search and rescue mission. He risked his life for a little cat lost in a gully.

Fluffy did not leave the kitten's side until it was out of the hole safe and sound. Then he walked proudly home with me.

Fifteen-year-old "Kitty," Fluffy's older sister, had not been feeling well. She left the house and laid down on the ground by the woods. Fluffy joined her and laid down beside her until she got up and came back into the house.

Whenever Fluffy's two baby brothers, "Blacky" and "Nelly," slip outside, Fluffy is right behind them until they are safely back in. Fluffy, our hero!

Fluffy and his younger brothers Blacky and Nelly sit by the porch door looking for new adventures. I look forward to writing about my "cat family" again in the near future.

Fluffy, Nelly and Blacky.